Unholy Worshipper

Moving from the Gifts to the Giver

James Levi, Ph.D.

Cover design & Publishing: Lifexcel Leadership
For more information visit: www.jameslevi.org
Email: lifexcelleadership@gmail.com

For Worldwide Distribution, Printed in India
1 2 3 4 5 6 /18 17 16 15

ISBN: 978-1-7344551-4-4

DEDICATION

This book is dedicated to all those who are unholy and yet still worship God. To the people who do not stop just at receiving the gifts but strive towards being with the giver.

CONTENTS

ACKNOWLEDGMENTS

Once again, I am grateful for a wonderful team of professionals who help me put this book together for you. Foremost is my publisher at Lifexcel Leadership. I also appreciate the designing and the marketing team.

In this book I've gathered many stories that I've heard from my friends and people I have met around the world. Thanks to all of them who have touched my life with their own. My desire in writing this book is to help you see what God is doing in, around and through you, so we become a blessing to bring glory to God.

I am grateful to my wife Annie and our children Saakshi and Namrata. They are my source of daily inspiration.

Now on his way to Jerusalem, Jesus traveled along the border between Samaria and Galilee. As he was going into a village, ten men who had leprosy met him. They stood at a distance and called out in a loud voice, "Jesus, Master, have pity on us!"

When he saw them, he said, "Go, show yourselves to the priests." And as they went, they were cleansed.

One of them, when he saw he was healed, came back, praising God in a loud voice. He threw himself at Jesus' feet and thanked him—and he was a Samaritan.

Jesus asked, "Were not all ten cleansed? Where are the other nine? Has no one returned to give praise to God except this foreigner?" Then he said to him, "Rise and go; your faith has made you well."

1

ALONG THE BORDERS

*Now on his way to Jerusalem, Jesus traveled along the border
between Samaria and Galilee.*

In No-Man's-Land

We didn't think we were lost—until we met this
group of people. It is amusing how sometimes we
think others are lost, when in fact it's the opposite.
Some of us friends had been planning an
adventure trip for a while and decided to go into
the wilderness close to the Himalayan mountains
where no one would be around. We wanted to be
away from all the whirr and buzz in the city as well
as far from our work pressure and deadlines, so we

found a remote place, far from any civilization. By the time we arrived at this no-man's-land, it was already dark. We set up the tent and got comfortable inside, ready for some well-deserved rest.

When we opened our eyes late the next morning, we were shocked by some strange-looking creatures staring at us. We were surrounded by some very curious goats. We didn't know it, but we had invaded their territory. But very soon we heard the noise of children playing, and as we looked up, we saw that a group of people were lodging nearby. After we ate our brunch, we walked up to this company of people to get to know them. They were nomads who lived and traveled along with their cattle and moved around depending on the seasons and time of the year. We also found out that these were the people who lived half of the year on our side of the country, and the other half, when the winter was severe, on the other side of the border, rearing their cattle and raising their families in another country. These people had the advantage of speaking the language of both countries, and they looked as though they could belong to either place. But soon we learned the harsh reality of their lives. In truth, they didn't belong anywhere. They couldn't identify with any one country or show solidarity with anyone. They were people left on their own. Neither country welcomed them. To others, they might as well not exist. They couldn't claim benefits or Social Security from anywhere. They had to protect and fend for themselves. They pay a hefty price for being people left in the in-between.

Many times this can be our spiritual condition. We don't know where we belong so we maintain our status in both worlds. We participate in worldly affairs as well as claim to be citizens of heaven. The fear of being committed to one keeps us far from anything and anyone.

Jesus Visits the No-Man's-Land

Jesus came to a place just like this no-man's-land. The scripture says he traveled to an area between the borders of Samaria and Galilee and went to a village which was sandwiched between them. There he saw a group of people who were outcast, abandoned and bereft of any identity. They were lepers and therefore a threat to society. No one wanted to take them in, they were not welcomed anywhere, and everyone was afraid of them. So, they were living on the borders with no claim on a place of their own. They lived in and around the margins.

But Jesus came to this place and met this group of people who were expelled from the community. He made space for these outcasts and time for these forgotten ones. Jesus met them because he understood the pain they were going through and he fully empathized with this group. Why would anyone go to this no-man's-land for these no-man's-people?

Jesus Longs for Those Who Don't Belong

These ten lepers lived in a village away from Galilee and Samaria because the people of these two places didn't want them there. They were living on the borders, homeless, insecure and discarded. When they talked among themselves, every word must have been filled with fear; they must have drowned in rejection and abandonment after being ejected from their community for bearing a disease in their bodies.

Maybe it was a beautiful morning when they found an abnormal spot on their skin while looking in the mirror. The next moment they were sitting in the priest's office waiting to be examined. The results came in sooner than expected and were positive for leprosy. From then on everything must have been both hazy and harrowing. They would no longer be near the people they loved. Everything changed. Their identity. Their relationships. Their value. Their purpose. Driven out, they were left only with fellow lepers. As long as they lived in that place, they were fine. But if they tried to return to their former life—it was over. The only thing they could do now was shake the memory of the past and adapt to this new reality, defined by what they carried on their body. Their illness now dictated their destiny. Imagine the anger, sadness, frustration, and hopelessness. One thing was certain: no one could change the condition they were in, nor could the community help them. What they needed was something bigger than themselves, bigger than their disease. Yet they found no solace, only sadness.

But then something happened. One day a Jewish rabbi named Jesus came walking to this border of Samaria and Galilee, the place where these lepers lived hidden. A dwelling where no one wanted to go for fear of contracting the deadly disease. Both groups (the lepers as well as those who rejected them) would meet in the middle (if it could be seen as a meeting), the ultimate social and physical distancing between them. Lepers helped the community by preventing the infection's spread by distancing. Townspeople responded by meeting their basic needs such as food and clothing. But they remained detached and disconnected. The gap could not be bridged. There was pain on both sides due to the separation.

Jesus' presence there was a radical step yet a powerful reminder that he understood the pain, separation and helplessness of these people. This also highlights a great truth about Jesus: He came to save the hopeless and hurting separated from the heavenly kingdom. That day, at the borders of Samaria and Galilee, Jesus not only healed the lepers of their sickness but he also bridged the gap between them and their people. God has created humanity to belong within a family and a community, as well as join the eternal kingdom. When we remain separated from him due to our sin, we feel that pain intensely. This bridge cannot be built by human effort, just like these lepers couldn't heal themselves. In the same way, humanity as a whole remained separated from a relationship with the living God until Jesus, God in human flesh, came to where others could not. His presence helps us to cross that vast gorge between us and God. This was a new dawn for those lepers who were hidden, marginalized and lonely for so long. God understands us, comes to us, abides near us and is for us.

He Identifies with Us When Our Identity Is Lost

Identity defines who we are, gives meaning to our self and names us. Identity situates us in a community as well as separates us as an individual. When identity is removed we dissolve into a nobody. When it is stolen or lost, something dies inside. Although these lepers were living together, they had lost everything from their previous life, their past, or what they were known for as individuals in the community. This new identity wasn't something they could get rid of, no matter how hard they wished. In the past they may have spent years cultivating their self-image and their unique identity through hard work, determination and with communal support. Looking back, they may say they were living the dream before the disease. Maybe the dream was to become famous or establish a large, profitable business, or perhaps marry their greatest love and raise a beautiful family. Others may just say they were *somebody*. But now they found all of that snatched away; things they valued and worked hard to build for their entire life disappeared. The community that supported them no longer had their back but instead were against them. How painful would that story be for anyone?

Maybe we have not experienced the effects of leprosy, but perhaps we have tasted other evils that are so prevalent in our society: racism, economic division, religious hatred, failed relationships, emotional wounds, devastating mistakes.

For some, this has created confusion and a loss of a sense of self. How strange would it feel for those who feel that they are living with a stranger in their own body, unable to recognize themselves. Not only has the community left you, but *you* have left you. You are a pile of broken pieces, a nobody. The disease had pushed them out of their known world and brought them to a strange community, away from their homes, their professions and the only life they knew and forced them to live with other outcasts in the same condition.

Does life make us feel the same way? Have you gone through a series of setbacks with no one to care for or understand you? Have you seen people who claim to know where they are going, but in fact, have no clue? Do we find ourselves surrounded by people confused, tired and disheartened with themselves, life and even religion?

The Lost Roy

Roy was one of the most exceptional people I knew when I was a young. He was a skilled carpenter with craftsmanship that set him above all the rest. He became very successful and well-known in his small town of a few thousand people. He made a good name for himself and with it came a lot of wealth. But he was also a generous man, who helped others in need and shared everything he had with great joy. Whenever he found the time, he would visit our home. And whenever he came, he came with a lot of money just to make us feel rich and be lavish with us kids. We always anticipated and enjoyed his visits. But then, Roy stopped coming to our house. We later found out that he had disappeared from his town. He was nowhere to be found. A few people who were close to him told us that he had gotten into a lot of debt and those to whom he owed money were after him. So, he vanished. He couldn't face his creditors or come back to his family. We never thought something like that could happen to a man like Roy. After many years I heard someone say that he was living in a faraway country with a different name and had started a new life. I haven't seen Roy since then, but I often think about how it might have been for him to lose everything: his name, his identity and everything he owned and was known for. Can someone rebuild and redeem after leaving everything behind? It reminded me of the lepers in that border village.

With complete knowledge of the lepers' situation and their suffering, Jesus walks up to them and gives them a place where they could once again belong. He came to create a new identity for those who had lost theirs. He came to give life. He came so that they didn't have to remain in that place of uncertainty and have a shattered identity forever. Christ saw more than disease. He saw people who were broken, people who were struggling to fit in, people who were desperate to see their family once again. He came to take away hopelessness and give meaning. Jesus came to their village and made himself available to those who were far and forsaken, to bring them near and accept them. A tremendous work was accomplished on the cross. It is an invitation to those who are separated from God to become a part of the eternal family. Jesus' presence at the borders of Galilee and Samaria was a presence that redeemed.

When Others Detach, God Attaches

Being uprooted from their good life to an abandoned one would lead to despair and mental distress. It may manifest as anger, fear, pain, and sadness, or all those emotions combined. In the company of strangers whose only common bond was disease, everything was amplified. Just the thought of being ripped away from one's spouse and little children can break anyone's sanity and result in unending tears.

What about the pain on the other side? What would a mother tell her little girl about her father, now forbidden in their home? Some may have tried to hide their loved ones for a while, but that didn't last long. Maybe one of the neighbors turned them in. How much anger would this family carry towards that neighbor, who was doing the righteous thing? How much stress and strain would this create? In the midst of this suffering, Jesus makes his way towards the village. Jesus appears near the camp of the abandoned and alone.

Perhaps someone spread the word that there is a man who has come near us, who heals the sick. Maybe someone came running through the camp with a message: "Our days of suffering will be over if we only cry out to him. This man has divine power—maybe he will have mercy on us. Others have rejected us and ejected us, maybe he will accept us and attach to us….maybe?"

These people had seen rejection often and in close quarters; their hopes have been crushed and betrayed by those whom they trusted. For the lepers, the priest made that final call, that ultimate judgment confirming the sickness. The religious leaders were seen as the cause of their pain and the fracturing of their families. In our pain, we will always find someone to blame. But does it help?

Few may have taken it upon themselves to see who this rabbi is. For some, it might have been hard to believe they could be cleansed. For others, there was nothing to lose by just showing up. There was nothing wrong in trying just one more time. They knew deep within their hearts that staying where they are was not a good option. Being away from their community and their loved ones was too much not to give it one more shot. They knew very well that being separated from their loved ones was not the way they wanted to live. With this in mind, they stood up as soon as they heard the call. These few felt deep within them that God could make things better and maybe good things could happen even in the darkest moment of their life. This promise is offered in the Gospel of John 3:16, "For God so loved the world that he gave his only begotten son that whosoever believes in him should not perish but have eternal life." Even today the same God is seeking those who are lost and lonely to give them an abundant life.

Jesus made a conscious choice to come near and appear to the disappeared. No one ever visited this village—it was a cursed place—but for Jesus, it was a village where God would birth beauty. Therefore, he attached himself to the detached.

Why did Jesus choose to travel to these borders?

Jesus Cares

Jesus' presence at the borders indicates his heart for those who are helpless and hopeless, and shows that they are always in his sight. His coming was to show that their sickness did not define who they were to him. His coming told them that human labels were not his own. It was profound for Jesus to include this group of people who were found on the margins. Jesus showed how his heart is moved with the compassion of God for the ostracized. His coming near conveyed an essential message: God is close to anyone who is forgotten or forsaken, for whatever reason.

Old and Alone

While traveling, I met an elderly woman who was living with her three young grandchildren. She was very poor and lonely and was going through a difficult time. Her son had committed a grave crime and was sentenced to many years in prison. The wife of her son (the mother of her grandkids) had left her children and ran away with someone else when her husband went to prison. There was no one to care for these grandkids, so the grandma came to their rescue and in her old age took upon herself the duty to care for the children. Though she was going through old age, sickness and struggle, when it came to caring for her grandkids she didn't think twice. To provide for the children, she labored hard in the field all day, day in and day out, yet it didn't deter her. She made a tremendous sacrifice because of the depth of her love. That's how God is; he will never abandon those who are discarded by others.

To Model Care

Jesus walking in the borderlands is a living invitation to all those who call upon him as Lord and Master to live and show the same kind of compassion and care. Oftentimes we avoid people who do not precisely meet our religious standards or belong within our group, but he compels us to welcome these forgotten people. His heart still longs for those who are excluded and it is crucial for us to walk with him where he is. We miss Jesus when we avoid the uncomfortable places where he is most often found.

His visit to the borders of Samaria and Galilee was a new model of how God works. Before that, it was usually defined by religious folks and human traditions of how to do spiritual work or execute the mission of God. However, Jesus shattered that paradigm. Jesus gave a new purpose to fulfill the heavenly mandate by inviting us to visit those who are living on the borders. He gave us a new vision for those in our midst who are lonely and excluded. He helps us to empathize with their pain. Jesus' visit not only healed the lepers at that moment in time but it echoed hope through the centuries and left a clear picture of how to emulate our Master.

Questions for Reflection:

- Describe a time in your life when you felt that you were living *along the borders.* Can you expressor share how and what you felt then?

- How have you seen Christ coming to your Borders/or share how you may have failed to see Him?

2

SEEING TO BE SEEN

They stood at a distance and called out in a loud voice, "Jesus, Master, have pity on us!"

The story doesn't stop with Jesus arriving where these ten lepers lived by themselves. He wasn't just present; Jesus *saw* them. He came near to see the ones who were hidden from the eyes of others. Jesus came to this place to *tell* these forgotten people that he sees them. The truth is God can see human suffering even without being there, but his presence near these lepers' dwelling was a powerful statement. Though they were invisible and rejected, Jesus saw and accepted them. How must the lepers have felt? Just to be seen is priceless.

Soccer Game

One evening I went to my daughter's soccer practice and she didn't know that I was coming to see her play. I didn't tell her because I wanted to surprise her. I arrived when she was already playing. I sat in the empty stands and watched her. She was on her average game until her eyes fell on the stands and saw a familiar figure there. As soon as we exchanged glances, she immediately felt a shift, which became evident on the field. As I watched her, it not only surprised her but now her game was different because she felt special. Her father was there—seeing her.

To be seen by someone who cares for you causes us to truly feel as if we are loved, valued and belong.

With Jesus at the borderlands, the lepers saw a pair of loving eyes gazing at them. Because of that they may have felt they are worthy of being seen. Because of that they might have thought that they are not as unclean as the rest of the world labeled them to be. Compassionate eyes start the healing process. Maybe these lepers thought they could hope for something better.

Remember the time you felt abandoned because you failed your loved ones or fell short of your own standards. Imagine in the midst of that someone with compassion rested their eyes upon you. Your countenance would change within minutes, and your heart and mind may have felt there were new possibilities. Well, that's what happened when Jesus the rabbi came to the borders of Samaria and Galilee and saw these lepers.

Maybe one of them got excited and told the rest, "Hey, someone is looking at us. Yes, seriously— someone out there is interested in us…just as we are." They would have been shocked just hearing those words. Or maybe that announcement may not have gone down well, and there may have been objections: "Well, no one has visited us for ages, and why would someone take an interest in seeing people like us? If they want to see anyone they should go to Samaria or Galilee, not here in the borderlands. I am not good enough to be seen." And someone must have thought, "Oh, they are here because they want to see what a leper looks like or get a picture for a charity brochure." But maybe a few got up and looked to see if what they were hearing was true. Deep in their hearts there was that desire to be noticed, to be seen and to be accepted—just as they are.

Don't we all have that longing to be seen even with our flaws and weakness? That deep longing didn't cease because of their sickness. One by one each of them came, and maybe with tears rolling down their cheeks, they saw a rabbi earnestly seeking and searching for each of them with a gentle, welcoming set of eyes. A loving look can bring forth healing in the heart of those who are condemned and rejected.

Girl from Captivity

My friend told me a story of a young girl who was rescued from a brothel in India. She was held captive by the sex-traffickers against her will for many years. When this young girl reentered normal society, it took a long time for her to believe that anyone could look at her with love, kindness, and joy rather than as a sex object or a toy. For years, her clients and her perpetrators saw her as someone to be abused. But once she knew she was safe and surrounded by kind people, every time someone looked at her, her eyes were filled with tears of joy. Just to be noticed for who she was—not for what she could be used for—was huge in this girl's life. It was deeply refreshing for her to be seen as a *person* and cared for after a long history of abuse.

Here in the story, Jesus didn't say anything to the lepers initially. He may have just come to their village and stood there silently, looking at each one of them with his eyes of tender care. That loving gaze brought some changes in that village.

They Felt Loved

That day, as these ten lepers who had not been seen by a compassionate eye for a very long time beheld the eyes of Jesus, it instantly changed their self-image. The world had rejected them and left them invisible, so they came to believe what they saw in people's eyes was true, that they were unqualified to ever be loved or seen as worthy. But today, as Jesus stood there and looked at them, it made them question everything that they believed in and the way they perceived themselves as others did. Jesus' eyes didn't stare at their flaws or disease but gazed deep into their being and saw what no one else could see. It set them free from within. At that moment, they felt love flowing through them;

they could not hold on to their rejection anymore. They surrendered themselves to this magnificent flood of love—loving them for who they were and not for what happened to them. Those kind eyes communicated that they were precious and priceless; those eyes said "I love you with an everlasting love. I not only care for each you but I am even willing to lay down my life for you. You do not know how valuable you are because you have allowed an already hurting world to define you as ruined. But I am inviting you to see the way God looks at you: beautiful, holy and precious."

This silent exchange spoke louder than any words could. It gave them value, hope and inner strength. The love seen through the eyes of Jesus penetrated their heart, mind, and soul and it caused them to live once again.

They Felt Hopeful

Hope is rarely created in isolation and can never be felt in the pool of rejection and abandonment. The people living on the border of Samaria and Galilee were abandoned because of the leprosy they had contracted in their bodies. The only thing they hoped for was not to see their life and body waste away. And many would have preferred death over the tragic life they were living. Until Jesus came and saw them. He didn't see disease, destruction or death but health, hope, and a future. The eyes of Jesus helped them to see beyond their situation and to hope for a transformed life. As each of them was seen, loved and valued, they became confident that good was coming—and in fact, already had— come their way. That hope offered them a moment of freedom even though they still carried the disease in their bodies. Hope said, "It doesn't matter what you feel at the moment or what you have felt for years, you can have a different tomorrow because someone sees you differently than the world. And what he sees in you is bigger than what the world sees."

The lepers, with this new hope bubbling within them, were challenged out of the status quo and into action. Though outwardly they didn't see any change, deep inside they felt hope rising within them. A few of them may have said, "Yes, we can trust those caring eyes." Some stood up even with their weak bodies and said to each other, "Let's not waste time, let us cry out and see, let's cry out and believe what we feel in our souls." Something big happened. Something formed within them because of the hope found in those loving eyes.

They started seeing what Jesus was seeing, people who were more than what the disease defined, people with a better tomorrow, people with the possibility of a bright future. What those eyes led them to see made them cry out, reach out and led them to something new.

They Felt Challenged

Hope captivated people long rejected. Now the lepers couldn't sit in the same old place; hope was showing them things that had been buried for years because of the pain. Hope brushed away the dirt, tore down the hindrances and removed the blockages that stood in the way of their freedom. Big dreams were coming to life. Their spirits were recharged, their voices had returned. The disease had shut them down. But now what the world had robbed reappeared with a new force. For a long time they were silenced, thinking they didn't deserve anything good because of what had happened to them. for the first time hope challenged them to expect something greater than anything they had experienced in the past.

Those who had trembled in fear because of society's prejudice and banishment, drew near to Jesus unafraid and unabashedly crying out. They couldn't believe why they were making such a ruckus, they couldn't believe what they were saying, they couldn't even believe *why* they were acting this way. It must have felt crazy to ask for such an outlandish thing, but hope reminded them that they could receive something despite their foolishness, because of *who* was standing there. They didn't have to explain why they needed healing. They didn't give into shame or guilt or discouragement or putdowns. Instead, hope spoke fresh words of life. Negativity and condemnation vanished. And faith swept in like a hurricane. That look of compassion told them they were worthy of asking for such requests because they deserved to be healed.

Those eyes helped them deal with the painful rejection they had gone through in three ways.

Disarming Rejection

Jesus coming to the borders of Samaria and Galilee exposed and dispossessed humanity of its powerful weapon of rejection. It could only be understood in light of what Jesus endured in the later part of his life when he experienced the worst form of rejection from his own and even from his followers. The Gospel of John starts with a statement, "He came to his own, and his own received him not." Later, it says that when he was arrested and taken to be crucified, "they all left him." This rejection was part of his assignment. His ministry prepared him to enter and endure rejection so that he could bring acceptance to humanity at large. His encounter with the ten lepers, who had been rejected because of the disease was a serious issue for him. He sincerely came near to those who were rejected to experience their pain and to participate in their suffering in order to make the following three important points:

- Participating in others' suffering prepares us to embrace our rejection gracefully.
- Rejection loses its intensity when others come close and surround us.
- Rejection is real, hard and evil when combined with social isolation.

Jesus, God incarnate, knew that rejection is a reality, but he also knew that it was not something any human should endure alone. He knew how much it can affect one's spirit and mind and how much it can distort the image of God they carry and thus their ultimate belief in the Creator. Rejection works from the exterior and makes its way into the interior of a person. Once the rejection makes its residence in the inner being of a person, then that person loses self-value and self-respect. The person becomes a captive of their external environment or the oppressor. Jesus came close to the ostracized, participated in their rejection, and invited himself into their suffering. This was symbolic of what he would feel on the cross when he cried out with a loud voice, "Father, why have you rejected (forsaken) me." When it came to the rejection Jesus faced, he endured it alone. There was no support or relief. He who experienced the darkest and thickest cloud of abandonment is willing and able even now to come close to all those who are experiencing rejection in any form. He exchanges our rejection for his acceptance. The ten lepers would have cried out, "Will there be any respite from this rejection? Will there be anyone who will stand with us?" The community had slammed the door on these lepers, expecting them to heal themselves and banishing them from the presence of others. While the world expected them to first get healed and then be accepted, God accepted them first, just as they were, which led to their healing.

Disarming Danger

Tragedy intensifies when it is shared in community. Each leper may have shared their story. Maybe they had been a loving father…husband…son…wife…sister…brother …when they discovered the disease and in a moment lost everything. Suddenly, they were unwanted and dangerous to their own. The sickness yanked them from their home, ripped them from their lover's arms and classified them as a threat. Friendships were far removed, with no hope of being restored. Because they were considered unclean and dangerous, many must have left their loved ones without even a goodbye kiss. All of them would have wished this was just a bad dream. They were now high-risk, with notices posted everywhere. There was no place these lepers could hide.

Jesus makes his appearance into *this* neighborhood, into *this* world. His coming close to the lepers' habitation relayed a new message to the towns and villages of Samaria and Galilee: What religion deemed unsafe was now received by Jesus in love. The lepers who had long believed what others said about them paused and questioned what they had been told: "If this man is drawing near to us maybe we aren't the danger we've been labeled?" Jesus' coming close to the lepers removed the label of "dangerous," and replaced it with "accepted." Jesus had the courage to face the threat of the disease and disarm the dangerous ones and change them into beloved ones. Jesus' presence transformed their self-image once and for all—and transformed the community's image of them as well.

Sister Mary

A medical doctor who used to visit his patients in the villages came back one day and reported that an epidemic had spread throughout one of the villages. The news created such panic and fear among the locals that everyone abandoned the affected area for many days, leaving the sick behind and helpless. That's when a group of Christian missionaries led by Sister Mary came to tend to them. They knew it was a dangerous thing to do yet they went and cared for them. After many days of the missionaries nursing the patients, a doctor and medical team from outside the village worked up the courage to go there. The doctor said, "If this bold woman with the love of Christ had not reached there on time the whole village could have been wiped out because of the epidemic."

The life of Jesus still challenges the world to show courageous love to help the weak and to face our fears in times of danger. People had to recognize that the lepers needed a community to feel safe, sane and welcomed. That's why Jesus came to that village. His presence caused a community to witness true healing. Jesus recreated the lepers' sick bodies as well as recreated the community by fixing their distorted thinking.

Disarming Disunity

When a group is characterized as dangerous the result is immediate separation. Walls are erected around people, segregating and creating disunity. And that was exactly what was done by the people of Samaria and Galilee. Though the people of Samaria and Galilee didn't agree on many things, when it came to the lepers they had come to one and the same solution: cutting them off. Panic and confusion came by dividing the families and breaking their bonds. This separation left a permanent scar on their hearts and minds.

In the midst of this trauma, Jesus makes himself available. He knew full well the extent of the division, and he came with the power of love to remove the barrier. Jesus walked into the middle of the fear, rejection, and discord and brought peace, unity, and healing to the two warring groups.

Similarly, Jesus appeared into our world, to a suffering humanity that was separated by sin and through his death disarmed the disunity between fallen humanity and a Holy God by drawing near to those who were distanced. His presence showed how unity could be birthed between suffering people.

Sin Removed

Jesus made a clear statement as he walked into that village where the lepers labeled "sinners" lived. In that day and age, this disease was viewed as a mark of God's curse, as described in the Hebrew scriptures. Jesus, who was the embodiment of God, didn't distance himself but took the sin of man upon himself and walked to the cross making it plain to both the religious and rejected that he can redeem. His coming showed that sin does not have the final say, rather God's mercy does. His presence declares that God forgives and accepts anyone. The lepers who were cleansed that day testified that their life heading towards destruction was rerouted by the power of God and his redemptive act.

Recreating Value

The world subscribes to success, strength, and skill but when you are weak, sick, and a failure you are often ignored, hidden and abandoned. Jesus' coming to this leper community was a rousing shout that with God it's not about success and strength; instead, it's about God's longing for the lost. He is there for those pushed to the sidelines by the world, which in its selfish race to get ahead, uses and abuses people. As long as they are healthy and useful, the world is good to them, but the moment they see them as weak and sick, they discard and trash them. But God comes seeking the discarded. He creates room for the marginalized. He believes in us even when we don't trust ourselves. He cheers for us. He hopes for us. That day, the lepers living on the borders were a testimony of God's longing and God's love.

Questions for Reflection:

- Describe an event or an experience where you felt that someone noticed you or saw you for who you are or maybe someone ignored you? How did you feel? What was your emotion?

- What are some areas in your life that is still facing the rejection? Describe the separation that you are experiencing because of this rejection (the way these ten lepers were experiencing separation due to the disease)?

3

HEALING PROCESS

They stood at a distance and called out in a loud voice, "Jesus, Master, have pity on us!" When he saw them, he said, "Go, show yourselves to the priests." And as they went, they were cleansed.

The healing we see in this passage is quite an unusual one. Jesus just asks the lepers to go and show themselves to the priest to be examined. He didn't touch them; he didn't say they were healed. He simply asked them to do something and when they obeyed, they were healed. We can note a few things about the healing this group experienced:

1. Jesus uses different ways to heal people. There is not a single definitive formula God uses to heal people. Maybe there was a reason why he

healed this group this way. At other times and in other places, Jesus healed with one touch, and for others he just spoke and sent the sick away healed. *It is important to trust God in the process.*

2. Healing is not restricted to a few or only for those who are righteous, but it is freely given and given unlimitedly to as many as needs it. No one can limit God's healing.

3. Though the healing has taken place, Jesus still wants people to have confirmation. He follows through with the procedure laid out by the Jewish leaders. He didn't violate the law or customs, rather he fulfills it.

Although it was Jesus who healed this group of lepers who were living in between Samaria and Galilee, there were certain things that they did so that they wouldn't miss the healing made available to them.

The lepers did three things when they saw Jesus coming to their village:

- Came Out

- Cried Out
- Went Out

Let us look carefully at each of these actions and see the implications for our lives now.

Came Out

The lepers came out and met Jesus. They stood at a distance, but still they came where they would be visible to him. They didn't stay away because of their disease, their shame, and their discouragement. Even though it was embarrassing to expose their illness in the full light of day, despite the unease and discomfort, they still came out. For so long society had rendered them invisible. Some of the lepers may have preferred that as they didn't want their sick bodies on display.

We often want to present our best to others. In doing so we often cultivate an image that is not reflective of who we really are. But to highlight our weakness and to be vulnerable with our brokenness and come to a place of self-acceptance just as we are, in whatever situation we find ourselves—that is the path towards our healing. These lepers were coming to a stranger, their sickness there for all to see. However difficult it may be, we must be willing to see ourselves in the lepers' place.

How often can we be courageous enough to open our wounds and share our pain with a stranger? How often have we hidden our shame, cloaking ourselves in leaves like in Eden? Many times we are our own hindrance to healing. Not that we should expose our weakness to the entire world, but living with our guard up never helps. So for these lepers, it was a step of courage, to come out and stand exposed just as they were. Being seen by Jesus was important enough for them to come out for all to see. Despite their weakness, their brokenness and their sickness, for once they were unafraid to be seen. This is a place, a moment where we accept our broken self, where the power of shame is undone, and the spirit of healing is released.

Thomas' Story

Thomas remembers his childhood with a smile. He was born in a religious home and surrounded by a strong faith community. He takes great pride in saying that he never missed any of his Sunday school classes at the local parish he attended with his parents. But Thomas did miss one important message: that it is OK to be who you are as well as to seek the help of others when we fall short of our standards. In his attempt to be perfect and whole, there were many things he kept covered, buried deep within him, inaccessible to all and unaware of it himself. However, years later he couldn't hide. So he moved out and made himself invisible to the world. It was a long journey of hide and seek until he couldn't do it anymore and sought help. There were things that surfaced in his behavior which affected his relationship with his fiancée and prompted him to get counseling. He did. And for the first time, he shared his heart. When he was willing to be vulnerable with another human in a safe space, he saw within himself things that he never knew were there. It took many sessions but slowly Thomas was able to unpack his emotional baggage and connect the dots between his past and his present choices and behaviors. Over time he was able to find the courage and willingness to arrive at a better place. Thomas needed truth, transparency and a safe place in order to begin the process of inner healing.

Do we provide those who are hurting within our community a safe place to be able to be vulnerable with all their bruises and scars? Or has our self-righteous image cast away many of those so-called "lepers" from our midst?

Jesus coming out and meeting these people provided a safe environment where those once outcast could now be out in the open. They didn't try to hide inside their shame and pain. They felt welcomed.

Cried Out

No doubt it is an act of faith and courage to stand exposed before others. But it takes an extra step forward to give honest expression to your feelings. Your fears, your shame, your helplessness all slowly find words to be spoken. Unless you speak, others' voices and opinions will dominate your condition. Once you speak up, you silence naysayers who belittle and discourage you. To stay silent is to maintain the status quo. To be healed, you must declare your dreams just as you acknowledge your sickness and true condition. Denial is not an option when it comes to healing. When you own it and announce that you are moving from that place of suffering, you make it clear to yourself and to others that you are ready to move to a new level and possess something better that God has for you. Above all, you are connecting to what God has always planned for you and has envisioned for so long. You are becoming his story. That is where you find true comfort and your hope is renewed. What you were ashamed to voice before, now finds a new strength, a place of acceptance, a clear understanding, and divine courage. The God who is with you hears the cry rising from your deepest place of fear, shame, and anger and leads you to a different path—but one that has always been yours.

These lepers, not only came out and met Jesus by standing at a distance, but they cried out together, to be set free and to be healed. And in that place of being together in their need, experiencing that suffering together in a community, something miraculous happened. Something that somehow took them to a place where it was no longer a personal healing that they desired, but now it was a common call for everyone's healing, a desire for communal wholeness. This cry is far and above the healing that we petition for ourselves. Here the prayer is no longer a laundry list but a plea for a greater anointing upon the community. Now you become part of a bigger need, you participate and speak up for *our* healing rather than just for *yours*. You feel and share what others are going through. Your cry is on behalf of your neighbor, as your heart connects with their loss or pain. You understand them, you reach out to hold them close, you are not ashamed to stretch your hands to wipe away their tears and to both mourn together. It is also a cry of intimacy. It is a voice making an unselfish human request, asking God to intervene in our dark world. It is faith that seeks justice in the midst of the brokenness. We ask him to come and set things right. We hold each other's hand and jointly seek mercy and healing. We ask for forgiveness. No longer is it just about my needs. The cry comes from an aching in us all.

It is important that your cry for help or healing is louder than the cry of just your pain. May you become a spokesperson for more than just your cause.

Went Out

The lepers came out from their houses, met Jesus who came into their village, cried out to him for healing and when he asked them to go and show themselves to the priest, they went.

The normal response could have been to stop and examine themselves and to ask Jesus why was there no sign of healing and what were they supposed to show the priest? But none of them took that route. They just went as they were told. It is not clear why no one doubted or asked for a sign. What made them have the faith to simply obey and go to the priest and show themselves when none of them were healed yet? What made them take that step when there was no evidence to support it?

Maybe for them it didn't matter. Or maybe they were in such a desperate place, they were willing to grasp any shred of hope. Even without any evidence of healing or any history of a leper ever being cleansed from that place, these people just took Jesus at his word. Was it an act of desperation or an act of faith? They had been desperate for healing for quite some time and nothing had changed, therefore this can only be seen as an act of faith.

It is a faith that follows vulnerability and openness, exposure and a willingness to be marked a fool by the world. It is a faith where shame is overcome by not being satisfied with the status quo. It is the faith of a community coming together and crying out for collective deliverance. It's the kind of faith that moves a mountain and with which people expect the impossible. Faith where all doubts are gone, and one is compelled to believe and to trust every word that is spoken from the mouth of the Lord. That's the kind of faith that doesn't ask for confirmation or argue for evidence.

Here there was something more significant than the mind involved. This was a matter of the heart. They knew that to possess the impossible they must close the textbook and silence the world's voice. This was a faith walk for them, and they were willing to go without any proof. They went after healing with just the words that had proceeded from the mouth of the Lord. Those words now resided in their hearts. They went. And on their way, they were all healed.

The scripture mentions that ten people who were lepers were healed, but we do not know how many lepers actually lived there in that village. How many of them did not come out to meet Jesus? Some of them may have just stayed back or been too lazy or too tired to get up and go...*for something that would change their life*. A few may have thought that it wasn't right for them to come and be exposed. They didn't want others to look at their diseased body. Their shame and pain may have held them back. And some may have come out and seen the rabbi, but because of their bitter history with religious folks they didn't believe or didn't cry out. For them, it was difficult to believe that someone like this could solve a problem like this. Maybe that's what caused them to go back and stay in their beds. And maybe a few others did come out and did cry out, but when they didn't see any sign of healing in their bodies, questioned it and went back. They didn't want to embarrass themselves by going to the priest only to find that nothing had changed. They didn't want to make a fool of themselves, so they got upset and returned to their houses. They were more willing to suffer the effects of disease than to step out in faith.

But that story would have changed as soon as those who were healed returned. Or maybe they never came back and went to the families they had left behind. Those who doubted and missed the healing might have wept. They might have thought, "Why did we ask all those questions and make fools of ourselves?" They may have thought the embarrassment in front of the priest would have been worth it. Maybe one of them said through his tears, "I'd rather be a fool and arrive at my destiny, then stay back and miss the miracle."

Healing Follows Obedience

The lepers didn't experience the healing initially or even when they started their journey, but they were healed as they went to the priest. What prompted them to go? The only thing they had was a word of Jesus. If someone had asked them along the way where they were going, and they told them they were going to see the priest to confirm their healing, they would have been mocked and scorned. That would have been discouraging.

The road to healing is not easy; it can be disappointing if we listen to other voices rather than keeping our eyes focused and ears attuned to the one who sent us. If they looked at their body for physical evidence they would have been disheartened. The only thing that kept them going were those words in their heart. The way to the priest became a path towards their healing. For that, they had to do the following:

- They had to obey Jesus' word rather than look for evidence.

- They had to keep going forward even when doubt crept in. Turning back was not an option.

- They had to come to a place where except for Jesus' word, there was nothing else to depend on—not even logic.

- When walking the lonely path, it is essential to have others to support your faith.

Healing is Different for Each Person

The way God heals people is unique in each case. We don't know if all of them were healed together in one instance. Maybe a few got healed first and then the others followed. How would those who were healed and those who weren't have responded along the way? Those who were healed may have tried to explain what they might have done to get the healing (though the healing didn't happen by their effort). Maybe for the sake of explanation some might have taken some credit for it. Or maybe one who was healed was compassionate and tried to help the others to keep going and keep believing what Jesus said—that they would be healed. The healed ones might have come alongside those who were yet to be healed to keep marching on. Maybe someone's healing may not have occurred until or just before he reached the priest's office.

Isn't it hard to see everyone healed except you? When others are marching on with healed bodies, and you are still sick? How would you feel to remain in the past when others have moved on? How can you walk in the present while remaining in the past when other have reached the future?

How would you react when everyone else is getting blessed, and you are doubly rejected and ashamed?

In that moment of spiritual, emotional and physical struggle, the only thing that you have are the words spoken by Jesus. You have to go on and keep believing for your healing. Even when the rest have moved ahead, you cannot allow self-doubt or discouragement to set in; you have to walk towards your healing. The word you received is equally powerful as what others have heard.

It's not a competition of who gets the healing first or when one is healed. It is a journey that requires us to keep moving. The word is received from Jesus as a community, but the healing might happen differently for each person. Maybe for one the healing was instant, and for another it was gradual. In all of it, God works with each of us individually to help us believe that he is in charge and he has a unique plan for each one of us. Only Jesus knows the what and the why. Someone may have wanted Jesus to just touch them and remove the leprosy and heal them, just as he had done to another leper in another gospel. But that's not how Jesus did it this time. This was an exceptional way of healing this community. He wanted them to take a journey as a group to the priest and on the way receive the healing.

We cannot dictate the terms of our healing nor can we demand the manner in which we get it. Instead, we have to submit to God's authority and his sovereignty in dealing with us the way He chooses, trusting it is the best pathway towards our wholeness and holiness. God wants us to come to that place of accepting him to be the Lord of our lives and allow him to work with us (and in us) in the way he thinks is best for us.

If we can trust that God can heal us then can we also trust his method?

Healing Has a Bigger Purpose

Many times our encounter with God is a short-term engagement. We just want to move on. But the very reason God reaches out to us is to establish a long-term relationship and deep friendship. But we often come with our own agenda and try to strong-arm God or get things out of him. Once that is achieved we express our hurried gratitude and wait for the next need to arise or crisis to happen to seek him out.

God relates to us differently than the way we do to him. He doesn't need us but he knows very well that we need him, not only to answer our requests but we need him to sustain our very breath. Maybe one of the reasons those needs arise is so that we understand the significant purpose behind our life. Living the good life or always being happy in this world is not what is most important. What is most important is how we connect with God and make this journey of life a meaningful, enriching experience, as well as everlasting, leading into eternity. That is all that matters. One of the reasons Jesus came to this village was because he knew in their suffering they would be more open to see him for who he is, rather than being occupied with their former lives and careers. Healing was the medium through which he was trying to commune with their heart and to make his permanent residence there. But were they able to see it? Are we able to see who God is and what he is doing in us and through us? Or do we miss out and miss him?

The Healer Sees the Healing in the Sickness

These lepers who came to Jesus with their sickness remained at a distance and cried out for healing. All Jesus says to them is, "Go and show yourselves to the priest." That's it. There was no preaching, or teaching or even praying. Even after that, nothing changed. Their bodies were still covered with leprosy as they stood in front of him. But he is asking them to go as if they have already been healed. He is telling them to show themselves to the priest as if the cleansing was complete. What is Jesus trying to convey here?

- Jesus speaks healing before it even begins

- Jesus can see what others cannot see
- Jesus calls out what is not yet as if it is already there; he calls the unfinished finished

If we are to work with God, it is important to see his ways of seeing and understand the ways he acts. Our world and our limited humanity mean we operate by our senses, but when it comes to comprehending the way God works in our lives and our world we must see him for who he is. He brings what is not into being. We are occupied with our human dimension but God is not bound by human limitations. These people were sick. But Jesus was able to see the complete work, and then confidently call it out. There was no fear, and there was no doubt. His work just confirms his power and his conviction in what he says.

Healing Respects Authority

Jesus healed the lepers, but he did it in a manner that did not upset the people in authority. Rather, he showed them the respect they were due.

He wanted the lepers to go and show their cleansed bodies to the priest. Jesus didn't want to overrule the office of the priest because he knew that it was important that those in authority be appreciated for taking care of the community. The healing was not complete until the priests were done with their work. Jesus included them. He invited them to be part of the process of what he was doing. His ministry wasn't exclusive. He welcomed others to become agents in the healing process. He was including the community in this new thing that God was doing. Something that would prepare them to expect and see things in a new way, God's way.

Many of them thought the day wouldn't come when these priests would confirm these lepers as clean. Priests were accustomed to pronouncing people unclean; it was the rare occurrence that these people were healed. There must have been a saying along the lines of, "Once a leper, always a leper." But this act of Jesus challenged that mindset. He wanted people to expect new things. He wanted to challenge the worldview of the religious people who had eroded the work of God from the community. He was spreading hope into every segment of society. The lepers were experiencing this new day, but so was the priest community. They had to re-examine their paradigm, and be ready to see things in a different light. By asking the lepers to go to the priest for examination, Jesus respected them and worked within the proper order of their society. He didn't replace their power but in fact, empowered them to have the final say in these people's futures. Though it was solely a God act, the community was involved in the process of healing. The same people who were authorized to exclude these people later become the people who accepted them into the community. Jesus still initiates such reconciliation through his work and his community.

Healing Can Be a Process

Jesus was highlighting an important concept here by showing that healing is often a process, which involves tracing the steps that brought them into captivity. God's power is free and can be instantaneous. But for the sake of people's awareness and as an explanation of the healing, it is good for a person to go through a process. To allow themselves to be examined by the priest. To wait to be pronounced clean or unclean. To go through the stages that are determined by the community so that they know what they have received. It helps instill gratitude for their deliverance, as well as strengthen their faith that what they have received is real and authentic. Going through a process slows us down, causing us to reflect and experience God in a way we couldn't if it happened in an instant.

Questions for Reflection:

- What does it means to be seen for who you really are? Do you feel afraid being authentic sometimes? What are your fears?

- Where or what area in your life do you want God to heal you? What are some fears that is stopping your healing?

4

THINGS THAT MATTER

When he saw them, he said, "Go, show yourselves to the priests." And as they went, they were cleansed.

Healing over Healer

The lepers were asked to go to the priest and show themselves as clean. When they started their journey, they weren't yet clean, but the scripture says that as they went on their way, they were healed. When was that moment? When did they look at themselves and see they were transformed? They weren't the same as when they had started—their appearance was changed. At that moment of recognition, there must have been a shout of joy, a sudden burst of tears and unspeakable happiness as they watched each other made new right in front of their eyes. This was a communal makeover on the road to the temple. They couldn't contain the excitement of all the future possibilities that were now open to them. Many wanted to hurry to the priest for their certificate of health and then return to their families, from whom they had been separated from for so long. They didn't want to waste a moment. This group of people formerly known as lepers rushed to meet the priest, running with eager joy.

We see that just one person slows down. The other nine who had walked so many journeys with him may have been taken aback that he had slowed down. They may have tried to drag him along with them to keep up at their pace and stay headed in the direction they were supposed to go. But instead, this man stopped, turned around and started going back to where he came from. The rest of the group was certain he was crazy. They may have shouted at him and insisted he come with them to the temple to be pronounced clean. They tried convincing him that it was important for him to get certified or else he would still be considered unclean.

But against the pressure of the majority, this man decided to continue on his way back. Baffled, the group finally let him go. He was on his own. He didn't belong. They might have pitied him. They must have thought he was ignorant of the proper procedure of being made clean.

Why did he turn back? What made him abort this important journey to see the priest? One of the greatest miracles had just occurred, but he chooses not to complete it? His answer is: "I am healed, but I want to thank the healer. The one who came looking for me and changed me when no one would come near and do what he did." For him, it was important to go back and express what it meant to him and to show how grateful he was for Jesus' compassion. Others were overwhelmed by what had happened to them. He was not only overcome by *what* had happened, but by *why* it happened to and *by whom*, so he couldn't help but turn back.

While the rest of them saw the healing as a random act of kindness, for this man, it was a kind act of God, not luck. While the rest were gracious regarding the gift they received, he was captivated by the grace of the giver. He couldn't proceed with his journey. Further, he couldn't stay with the crowd any longer. Though lonely, he went back to where he came from. He had to visit the place where it all began and meet the one who had changed his reality. His answers as to why he went back may be as follows:

The Healer Is More Important Than the Healing

It was indeed a blessing to receive healing and indeed unbelievable, but his coming back said something about him and what he valued. For him, healing was fantastic. But the one who healed him was far more valuable. For him, the gift was significant. Yet meeting the giver of the gift was far more important. He understood the difference between the effect and the cause. While the group that was healed grabbed the healing and rushed forward, he had to connect his healing to the source. What made him feel that was important? He couldn't think of continuing his journey without meeting the healer first. For the others, the healer was the means to their healing. For him, the healing was the means to the healer.

There was a vast difference between his perspective and theirs. While the healing was distant, all of them looked the same—sick and diseased. But healing revealed what was beneath and brought it to the surface. While others could receive the healing and just forget the healer, he could not. This man distinguished between what the healing had done to him versus what the healer did to him. Healing didn't take away the healer but brought him near. Until then he may have heard about healers, but never encountered one.

Healing was not his final destination; it was a route to reach his healer. The one who came looking for him is now the one he went looking for. Others were looking for completion when they saw the priest. This man wouldn't be complete until he met the healer. So he went back.

Healer Before the Crowd

It wasn't easy to free himself from the crowd or turn away from the rest of the nine who had decided to go to the priest. To pull himself away and take the road back to the healer was a lonely one. He wasn't part of the community anymore. These were the people who were with him when he was suffering from severe sickness; they identified with him. These were the people who had stayed and comforted him. But now he parted ways with them.

It must have been an emotional farewell to choose the healer over those who walked with you from sickness to health. It couldn't have been easy. They were the ones who knew him the best, they were the ones who stayed with him the longest. Now he was choosing someone he just met a moment ago over them. There was nothing he had in common with the healer. His history was shared with the nine. But the healing made all the difference.

What must be going through his mind? How would he have handled the wave of loneliness that came over him? Maybe the joy of healing might have turned bittersweet as he walked alone, leaving all his friends and their celebration. When everybody was moving forward, he moved backward. Others may have gone to the priest and went on with their lives with family and friends, but he was left alone. There were no good reasons to decide as he did. But there was a deep longing within him that he wanted to fulfill: to worship. Healing revealed something greater. It connected him to something bigger. This was someone he didn't want to miss, this was someone who was out of this world. He knew what happened to him—the healing—and what lay ahead of him—a visit to the priest and a return to his former life—were far less in value than what was behind him. His healer. He had to meet him.

Presence Over Presents

Now for the others, the future had cracked open right in front of their eyes. They had lost years and now was the time to redeem the time. They couldn't waste a moment. So much had been lost. They had missed their loved ones so much. There were things to buy and to build, to create and to cultivate. Now they were ready. They were ready for forward action. All except one man. For him, time with the healer was what was most precious. With this in mind, he went back. The disease had taken away everything in their lives, and the others couldn't afford to waste time. But this one man had no time to waste anywhere except with his healer. Though his sickness was no more and that was a tremendous gift, he was full of wonder regarding something else. The healer had made time for them, but this man made time for the healer. He didn't want to be anywhere except the healer's presence.

We don't know how he came to choose worship over the healing, the healer over the crowd, and presence over the present of healing deemed so precious by the world. He must have had ample opportunities to seriously reflect on life, what mattered and what didn't. He must have come to a place of understanding that nothing is more important than knowing who God is and finding him and being in his presence. It is above and beyond anything else he could be or have.

Questions for Reflection:

- According to you what must be going through the mind of the man who returned to meet Jesus leaving the group ? How do you think he would have handled the sudden loneliness that came to him on his way back?

- Why do we sometimes get so focused on our healing than the healer?

- Would we be ever okay to have the healer without the healing or do we prefer just the healing without a healer?

5

RETURN OF THE UNHOLY ONE

One of them, when he saw he was healed, came back, praising God in a loud voice.

As soon as the man returns and sees Jesus, he falls at his feet and worships him. He expresses his heartfelt thanks for what the healer did for him. Though he was alone, he didn't restrain his gratitude towards the healer. He worshipped him wholeheartedly. He praised him continuously. He was the odd man out offering worship.

But then he heard the healer ask for the others who were healed. Jesus was surprised to see just one of them return to give thanks. Now this former leper understood something. He thought this man just went around and healed people. But in fact he was seeking a deeper relationship and connection with people. At first, he was surprised to find the healer waiting for him, but then a few things became clear:

He Waits for Them

It was a revelation for him to know that the healer was not just interested in healing the people, but he was interested in the people themselves. He lingered, he didn't leave. He waited for the ones who were healed. He had time for the healed just as he had time for the sick. Others said the healer was busy as there were so many people who needed healing—this one man wasn't his sole interest. But seeing the healer still standing there told him otherwise. The others had got this healer all wrong. There was more to him than miracles. He wanted to commune.

Because this man came back, and was willing to resist the crowd, he was able to know the heart of the healer. He learned that the healer saw beyond disease and saw a precious child of God. The disease neither attracted nor distracted him. He was so in love with people just the way they were that he was willing to die for them. The man who came back got it. The others failed to see it. This man connected with the healer beyond just his point of need. He saw something bigger and deeper.

He Is Interested in Each One of Them

Another truth that this unholy worshipper, a Samaritan, discovered was that the healer was interested in each one of them. He was not there just to see how many lepers were in need of healing but he also wanted to know how they felt when they were healed. This is a God who wants to connect with us in our deepest moment of pain and in our sweetest moments, too. Jesus' desire was that once they were healed of their sickness they would know that there is something still missing. He wanted to be there for them. He knows each one he heals because he asked, "Was this Samaritan the only one who came back?" God is well aware of who we are, where we are and what is going on in our lives.

This healer had an expectation. He wanted them to return. Why was that? Was it because he wanted to feel good about himself? Or was it because he thought that a community that is grateful experiences a deeper life? The healer's question had great meaning. It was not about him, but it was for the sake of these people. There was something they wouldn't have understood at the time of their sickness that he wanted to reveal to them when they were healed. He knew people's outlooks on life change when they experience good. If that moment is consciously connected to God, then it can create something beautiful.

He Is in Search of a Thankful Heart

The Samaritan returns to offer gratitude at the same place he had left as a leper. He is surprised to find the healer waiting for him at just the right place. On his lonely walk back it may have looked like he was doing the wrong thing. But when he saw the healer, he knew that he was in the right place. What made him feel that way? What was so important about being here?

I believe Jesus was looking for worshippers and he was glad to find one. A grateful heart would move one beyond the place of healing to that of worship and allowed one to meet God in a different way. Jesus wanted each of them to experience what he had come to offer, but nine of them took what they thought was enough. They stopped at the healing when Christ was willing to offer so much more.

Jesus knew when people are in need, outcast, abandoned and desperate like these lepers were, they needed hope. They needed someone to reach out to them and help them. That could only happen when those who received that help and healing had grateful hearts that led them to true worship of God. Jesus was there ready to give holistic healing. But nine of them were satisfied with physical healing alone.

The one who came back was now called a worshipper of the living God. He went from being a healed man to a worshipping man. His life's marker was not when he got healed but when he worshipped. That was the event that defined him.

Questions for Reflection:

- Why did you think Jesus waited for the man to come back to give thanks? Why was it important for Jesus to ask about the *other nine?*

- When others saw the *healer in their time of need, the man who came back to Jesus to give thanks could see the healer beyond his time of need* and enter into God's time for something bigger and deeper. Does it in any way apply in your life?

6

FAITH & WORSHIP

"Rise and go; your faith has made you well."

Worshipping God always means taking a different route than the crowd's. When we follow God there are often times we feel lonely and left behind. Those who supported us when we were seeking healing will leave us when we move into worship. The reason is that worship is centered not on our needs but on God's beauty and his character and his worthiness. Many seek God to fulfill a personal agenda; as soon as their needs are met, their search ends. You won't find many worshippers at the feet of Jesus. But this man, a Samaritan who was not well versed in worship tradition, is a true worshipper.

One thing that emerges out of this passage is that worship is not a learned behavior, it's an expression of the heart. You don't have to be religious to engage in worship. We don't need to know the correct rituals or practices because worship is not about "how to" but "who." Worship is about knowing the One who exchanged his life for ours. This poor man, a Samaritan who was considered unholy and far removed from the Jewish faith, found favor in the eyes of God as a true worshipper. He moved beyond celebrating the miracle to celebrating the miracle worker. That is true worship. How often does following God conclude once our goals are met rather than extend to find God and meet his goals? When we make it more about him than us, a mystery is revealed to us.

About that revelation…

- It often happens when we're alone rather than in a crowd
- It's more about God than us
- The revelation is not just for the mind, it has to flow from our heart as well
- Worship is not reserved for one group; anyone can connect to Him
- It is not about the right theology or location, but it's about the right person

In worship
- Mystery is revealed
- Truth is learned
- We learn what God thinks about us
- We know God as more than just a healer
- God converses with us
- We gain direction and vision for our life

These are a few things that this former leper, now a healed worshipper, understood as he worshipped Jesus. He also discovered the reason Jesus came to his village. While the nine thought

Jesus was a compassionate person who can heal, this one man came to know Jesus in a more profound way. He saw God on a personal level, unlike the nine who experienced him in a crowd. He experienced a truth which was revealed only in worship.

Faith

Jesus told this man, privately and personally that, "his faith has made him whole."

This unholy worshipper, once a leper and once rejected, learned something about faith that the others didn't. He now knows what moves mountains. He didn't just get healing, he received the truth that set him free forever—truth that revealed to him what faith can do. Faith in a God who is compassionate and willing to heal, one who is bigger than all of our problems, one who has come to give us abundant life, and one who came to bring light to a dark world. This faith meant he didn't stop as a receiver, he became a giver, too.

He didn't have to seek the physical Jesus anymore because he understood by faith he can reach him by the Spirit. He could ask anything, and that would be given by faith. The truth empowered him to live life differently even from his pre-leper life, and to live with a higher purpose. While the nine went back to who they were before, this man became something more. For this unholy worshipper, healing propelled him forward. His faith led him to a much larger mission: to be a worshipper of the living God.

Worship

The Samaritan, the former leper, become famous for his worship over the years. Not because of his healing or having been a leper, not even because of his beautiful worship style. He has become a classic example to all those who want to worship God in a way that touches his heart. All that requires is gratitude and a willingness to walk alone and seek God as our first order of business.

Throughout the years he has encouraged many people to find truth through his worship of God. Worship that transforms our lives to be used for a higher purpose. Worship that encourages others to enter into an intimate relationship with God.

Mission

Jesus told him "Go." He was sent as he worshipped. He received his mission, his purpose and his direction when he came back and worshipped God. While the others thought he was missing out and losing out, in reality he found himself. He knew what to do. He knew there was someone who asked him to go. He now had a purpose. There were no questions about returning or remaining, now he knew for sure what he was supposed to do because he was sent. He was sent with faith, carrying God within him and knowing His voice well. Unlike the nine, he would have direction whenever he felt lost. Worship led him to that place of clarity, strength, and mission.

Love

One of the best gifts this unholy worshipper received when he came back to offer his thanks was getting personal time with Jesus. Earlier he was one among the crowd. He didn't know if the healer knew him or even saw him in the group. But as he worshipped he learned this healer knew everything about him.

It was a sacred moment for him to be alone with the creator of the universe. The heavens stopped for him. He could now know how precious he was. Being with Jesus showed him that God was for him. Knowing this, he needn't worry anymore or fear tomorrow. He was strengthened by that presence and the knowledge that he was known by the God of the universe. Need brought them to God, but the nine couldn't see their need beyond healing. For the nine, their stories stopped once they saw the priest, and were healed, but the story of this man continued. For him, God become personal. His story had a conversation. His story was one of communion.

May we know God intimately just as this man knew him. May we like this unholy worshipper know there is more to this life than just us, our needs and our goals, and see the purpose that God has for us. May we always have a grateful heart and follow him even when the others leave. May his presence be real in your life. May we remember that *what* happens to us does not define us. Instead, *who* happens to us is what determines our past, present and future—and that is who we worship.

Questions for Reflection:

- What do you understand about faith, worship and mission from the above story?

- How have you worshiped God lately, how does your faith informs and affirms it?

- What mission is God calling you in this season of your life?

ABOUT THE AUTHOR

James Levi, Ph.D., is a Christian minister who regularly conducts retreat and workshops. He was born and raised in India. After completing his master's degree in biochemistry, he worked in the healthcare industry. Later, he felt called to pursue his calling. His Ph.D. is in international development with a specialization in leadership.

He is a licensed pilot who loves making coffee for his wife and spending time with his two daughters.

James Levi's other books are available on Amazon and you can also check his blogs and vlogs at www.jameslevi.org

Your feedback is very much appreciated at lifexcelleadership@gmail.com

www.ingramcontent.com/pod-product-compliance
Lightning Source LLC
Chambersburg PA
CBHW021133020426
42331CB00005B/747